# A STEP-BY-STEP BOOK ABOUT
# SEAHORSES

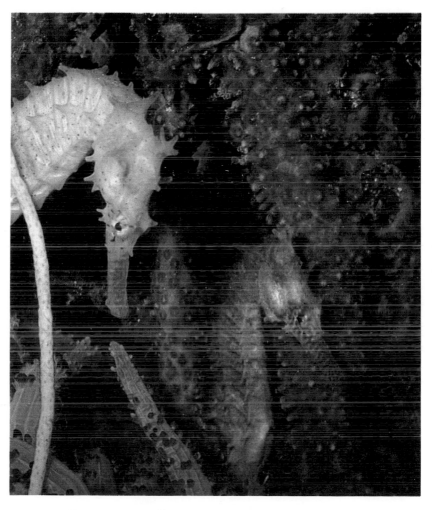

## PETER GIWOJNA

**Photography:** on title page and pages 7, 9, 10 (left), 23, 24, 27, 31, 32, 35, 36, 40, 42, 43, 44, 55, and 59 by Joel K. Giwojna, Lensmaster Photos. Other photos by Dr. Gerald R. Allen, Charles Arneson, Dr. Herbert R. Axelrod, Hilmar Hansen, Ken Lucas, Gerhard Marcuse, Marine Studios, Aaron Norman, courtesy Steinhart Aquarium, William M. Stephens.

**Humorous drawings by Andrew Prendimano.**

# ACKNOWLEDGMENTS

The author is deeply indebted to Joel Giwojna of *Carefree Aquariums* in Chanhassen, Minnesota, for providing many of the unusual specimens illustrated in this book, especially colorful invertebrates for miniature reef tanks. In addition, the author is equally grateful to Ben Giwojna for his invaluable assistance in feeding and caring for a herd of hungry seahorses.

*Dedicated to Kelly Swanson, a fellow nature lover and amateur naturalist, who shares my fascination with everything from hermit crabs to tarantulas and from snakes to seahorses.*

Distributed in the UNITED STATES by T.F.H. Publications, Inc., One T.F.H. Plaza, Neptune City, NJ 07753; in CANADA to the Pet Trade by H & L Pet Supplies Inc., 27 Kingston Crescent, Kitchener, Ontario N2B 2T6; Rolf C. Hagen Ltd., 3225 Sartelon Street, Montreal 382 Quebec; in CANADA to the Book Trade by Macmillan of Canada (A Division of Canada Publishing Corporation), 164 Commander Boulevard, Agincourt, Ontario M1S 3C7; in ENGLAND by T.F.H. Publications Limited, Cliveden House/Priors Way/Bray, Maidenhead, Berkshire SL6 2HP, England; in AUSTRALIA AND THE SOUTH PACIFIC by T.F.H. (Australia) Pty. Ltd., Box 149, Brookvale 2100 N.S.W., Australia; in NEW ZEALAND by Ross Haines & Son, Ltd., 18 Monmouth Street, Grey Lynn, Auckland 2, New Zealand; in the PHILIPPINES by Bio-Research, 5 Lippay Street, San Lorenzo Village, Makati Rizal; in SOUTH AFRICA by Multipet Pty. Ltd., 30 Turners Avenue, Durban 4001. Published by T.F.H. Publications, Inc. Manufactured in the United States of America by T.F.H. Publications, Inc.

# CONTENTS

# THE SEAHORSE

## Something for Everyone

For centuries people have been enthralled by the charming appearance, amusing antics, and strange behavior of the seahorse. Scientists, laymen, and aquarists alike are equally fascinated by these delightful creatures. Their many desirable qualities have made dwarf seahorses (*Hippocampus zosterae*) the most popular of all marine fishes, and they are probably responsible for converting more hobbyists into marine aquarists than any other species.

I have witnessed the irresistible appeal of the seahorse many times while showing my aquariums to friends. For example, my 70-gallon display tank houses a number of outstanding specimens: a spectacular 14-inch African lionfish, three feet of azure appetite better known as a blue ribbon eel, an overgrown panther grouper decorated with dime-sized polka dots, and a two-spotted octopus living in a queen conch shell, among others. A nearby 30-gallon community tank for smaller fishes is stocked with a similar assortment of coral beauties: a shocking pink and yellow royal gramma, a pair of clownfish, a flaming angelfish, a regal tang (which has been described as the bluest thing on Earth), a psychedelic-colored Mandarin goby, scarlet ladies, and a mated pair of pink and purple spotted harlequin shrimp.

After looking over all these aquatic gems, guess which one impressed my friends the most? Was it the life-and-death drama played out when the hungry lionfish, with his flowing mane and feathery fins fanned out to their fullest, snapped up his meal of live minnows the moment they darted out from the shelter of the coral? Or did they get their biggest thrill from hand feeding the octopus? Perhaps they were captivated by the puppy-like panther grouper that swims to the front of the aquarium wagging its tail whenever anyone approaches the tank, hoping for a handout. Or could one of the dazzling little jewels adorning my 30-gallon tank have caught their eye? Nope. Invariably, it was the brilliant orange seahorse that inspired the most "Oohs!" and "Aahs!"

**Facing page:** A trio of seahorses showing color variation. These three marine equines retained their natural coloration in the miniature reef, but others have been known to camouflage themselves.

And a rare beauty it was, too, colored a fluorescent orange that literally glowed under special lighting. But its stunning color was not what impressed them most. It was simply the fact that they were looking at a real, live seahorse that struck their fancy. Most of them had never seen one before. And they were enchanted. More than one of my friends have remarked that, if they could keep only one fish, it would be a seahorse.

This popularity is not surprising when you consider its many special features. Here is a fish with the head of a horse, the ability to change color like a chameleon, the prehensile tail of a monkey, an armor-plated body like an armadillo, a kangaroo's pouch, and turreted eyes like a lizard. Judging from its appearance, you get the idea that, on the eighth day of Creation, the Good Lord decided to put together all the spare parts and bits and pieces left over from the first seven days, and came up with the seahorse. Perhaps that's why there are still people who are firmly convinced that seahorses exist only in the realm of mythology, right beside mermaids and sea serpents. After all, an animal that combines all of the bizarre anatomical features of the seahorse does sound like the stuff of legends. Its appearance is so unusual that many people, including some aquarists, find it hard to believe the seahorse is actually a fish when they first see one. I've even had friends argue with me that my blazing orange specimen isn't really a fish—*while* they're admiring it swimming around in its tank!

It's easy to understand their confusion, for the seahorse is certainly the most unfishlike fish imaginable. But strange as its anatomy is, there are good reasons for the seahorse's peculiarities.

Take its bulging, lizard-like eyes, for instance. Independently operating eyes allow the seahorse to keep one eye peeled for potential predators while searching for food with the other. Being able to look both ways at once is a neat trick that naturally helps it both to avoid its enemies and to find its prey.

Further protection is provided by the seahorse's suit of armor. The body armor is composed of interlocking bony plates that form ridged rings where they join together. Tiny knobs and spines mark the joints where these plates fit together, so that its exoskeleton looks as if it is made of steel plates that have been bolted or riveted together. Underneath its ironclad exterior, the seahorse also has an internal skeleton like that of other fishes.

Just as its armored body helps protect it, the seahorse's prehensile tail serves an equally useful purpose. Unable to withstand strong currents, the seahorse has developed a grasping tail that it can wrap securely around sea grasses, gorgonians, coral, or any other handy objects. Once it "drops anchor" in this fashion, the seahorse is protected from the buffeting of the waves and tides. Moored safely in place, the seahorse spends most of its day resting, literally "lurking in the weeds," waiting for prey to pass within easy reach.

Animated chesspiece: knight to queen four? Seahorses easily remind one of living chessmen, as their hollow, elongated jaws give the head the appearance of a horse—or knight!

However, the seahorse has paid a price for this protection in terms of its mobility. Being encased in a bony exoskeleton and lacking a tail fin—the principle means of propulsion for most fishes—it is naturally a poor swimmer. In fact, it appears to glide majestically through the water as if by magic, with no visible effort whatsoever. Its miraculous means of locomotion can be discovered only through careful observation. Close examination will reveal a high-speed blur at the center of the seahorse's back. This is its nearly transparent dorsal fin, oscillating as fast as 20–30 times per second. The seahorse is thus propelled slowly through the water by the rippling action of its dorsal fin.

# The Seahorse

Once underway, steering is accomplished with the aid of its fan-like pectoral fins. The all but invisible pectorals look like tiny cellophane ears, and they function like miniature rudders or vertical stabilizers, permitting precise course changes. The seahorse is also able to move up and down simply by "flapping its ears" and "shifting its ballast"—curling up its tail to descend and straightening its tail when it wants to rise again.

Needless to say, this method of locomotion is necessarily slow. Although it gives the seahorse an effortless grace and stately dignity, it is useless when a quick getaway is required to escape from danger. Rather than outrunning its enemies, the seahorse is forced to rely on its armor and ability to camouflage itself to avoid harm.

Fortunately, it is truly a master of disguise. The seahorse has perfected the art of blending into its background, and its color changing ability would turn a chameleon green with envy. For example, the "normal" background coloration of the northern giant (*Hippocampus erectus*) is a dark brown or charcoal gray, but it frequently exhibits several other color phases ranging from snow white to jet black, and, when called for, it can also assume the most vivid of hues. Its background coloration is interrupted by a series of lighter streaks, spots, and blotches, which break up the silhouette or profile of the seahorse, further deceiving the eye.

Thus, if a seahorse has taken up residence in a bed of eel grass whose blades are heavily overgrown with calcareous encrustations, coralline algae, and hydroids, it will assume a mottled appearance that perfectly matches these growths. Consequently, a seahorse that lives among bright green grass is apt to be bright green in color, which accounts for the emerald and chartreuse specimens that sometimes turn up. Likewise, if it lives amid brownish or yellowish sea grasses, it will assume a color to match. More rarely, blazing orange and fiery red seahorses are found living in colonies of orange or red sponges. Only about one of these bright scarlet specimens is found for every 1000 *Hippocampus erectus* that are collected.

The results of a collecting expedition in Florida Bay provide a good illustration of color variations among seahorses. During this expedition, a single pass of the trawl over a bottom consisting mainly of manatee and turtle grasses produced a haul of 32 dwarf seahorses (*Hippocampus zosterae*). Included among these 32 pygmies were white, tan, chocolate brown, yellow, bright green, and golden individuals.

Such color changes are accomplished by expanding and contracting tiny pigment cells, or chromatophores, in the skin. The results

Seahorses are rather mellow creatures that enjoy companionship with compatible tankmates.

can be quite dramatic, as I discovered when I bought a pair of black Indian Ocean seahorses. This species is unusual in having yellow bands on its tail, which contrast nicely with its blackish background coloration. The new acquisitions quickly made themselves at home, feeding eagerly on live brine shrimp shortly after being introduced to the aquarium, and all seemed well when I went to bed that evening. The next morning, however, I was awakened with the alarming news that the seahorses were gone. Since they were the only inhabitants of a ten-gallon aquarium and couldn't possibly have escaped, I wasn't too concerned as I got up to see for myself. Sure enough, though, at first glance the tank looked empty. The three- to four-inch long seahorses should have been easy to spot, but after a quick search, they were nowhere to be seen. Upon closer examination, I noticed that one of the tines on the staghorn coral was striped with yellow, and all at once a *white* seahorse materialized before my very eyes. Now that I knew what to look for, I soon located the other snowy seahorse perched on a piece of finger coral. Anchored motionlessly in place, they seemed like natural extensions of the bleached coral. We could have gone on looking for *black* Indian Ocean seahorses all day, and never found them.

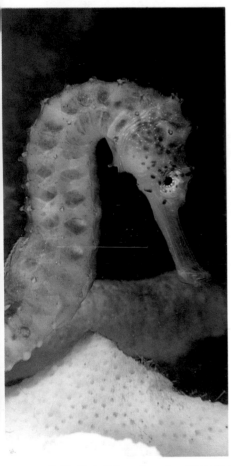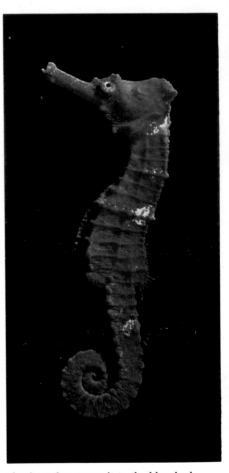

**Left:** Note this seahorse's whiter shade of pale and compare it to the blanched coral that surrounds it. **Right:** "Move me onto any black square." This unusually vermillion character is an example of one end of the seahorse spectrum.

Mildred Bellomy describes an even more striking example of this. During the holiday season, a ceramic Santa Claus was placed in an aquarium with five lined seahorses (*Hippocampus erectus*) as a sort of Christmas decoration. Over a period of about a week, one of the dark brown seahorses gradually turned bright red, retaining its fiery hue as long as the scarlet-robed Santa remained in the tank.

10

# The Seahorse

In addition to its color-changing ability, the seahorse further enhances its camouflage by displaying dermal cirri, which are branching spines or twig-like extensions on its head and body. The presence of such cirri is also a variable trait, depending on the seahorse's habitat. If its normal habitat is an unusually weedy or bushy environment, a seahorse is likely to have well-developed cirri, giving it a shaggy appearance. Other specimens from less "twiggy" surroundings will have tiny knobs only, rather than branching cirri.

When combined with its variable pigmentation, the ability to further disguise itself by forming cirri renders the seahorse all but invisible in its natural habitat. This vanishing act is so convincing that, even when they are collected by hand seining, seahorses are easily overlooked among the plant debris that accumulates in the net.

Somehow it seems only natural that these armored, monkey-tailed chameleons should come equipped with a kangaroo's pouch. Like the Australian marsupial, the seahorse incubates its young in a pouch, and they are fully developed when they emerge. With our fishy friend, however, it is the male who experiences the labor pains and delivers the young. By now it should come as no surprise that, like almost everything else about it, the seahorse also reproduces in a most unfishlike fashion.

When the Almighty was assembling the seahorse from His collection of spare parts and leftovers, He must have been fresh out of a few items, because the finished product was a fish with no teeth, no ribs, and no stomach. Since it swallows its food whole and has an iron-clad torso, the seahorse has little need for teeth or ribs. With no stomach to store food, its digestive tract consists of a simple alimentary canal and an intestinal system that is little more than a hollow, coiled tube. The seahorse compensates for this by feeding more or less continuously and consuming enormous amounts of food.

All things considered, the seahorse has more to offer aquarists than any other fish I can think of, for it is one wet pet that truly has something for everyone. For instance, the dwarf seahorse (*Hippocampus zosterae*) is perfect for the beginner. It's inexpensive, exceptionally hardy, and breeds readily in the aquarium. Keeping dwarves allows the novice to learn the basics of good aquarium management for a very modest investment, while greatly increasing his chances of success. On the other hand, more experienced aquarists will enjoy the challenge of breeding and raising the larger species of seahorses. And even the most advanced hobbyists can look forward to keeping seahorses in the new miniature reef setups, for which they are ideal inhabitants.

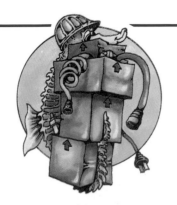

# EQUIPMENT
## THE SEAHORSE STABLE

The first step for those of you who would like to enjoy these enchanting creatures in your home is to prepare a suitable "stable" for your future pets. Since metal-framed tanks can poison marine fishes, your seahorse corral should be an all-glass or plastic aquarium. Almost any container composed of inert materials will do as long as it is filled with clean sea water, or a good brand of synthetic salt water, and equipped with an efficient filtration system to provide aeration and maintain optimum water quality.

If your space is limited and your aquarium budget is tight, the stable need not be at all large. For instance, with proper filtration, a five-gallon aquarium can comfortably house as many as 50 dwarf seahorses (*Hippocampus zosterae*), and a 2½-gallon tank will support up to two dozen pygmies. Likewise, a two-gallon drum-type goldfish bowl with a subsand filter makes a fine home for ten or twelve dwarf seahorses. In fact, I know one person who successfully kept a pair of pygmies in a king-sized brandy snifter. The snifter held about two to four quarts of salt water and was equipped with a subsand sponge filter. The pygmy ponies seemed perfectly healthy and happy in this unusual setup.

As for the larger seahorses, a 15-gallon aquarium is roomy enough for half a dozen adults. Given an efficient filtration system, a ten-gallon tank can easily support four large seahorses, and a five-gallon aquarium can comfortably house a pair of giants.

Seahorses are one of the few marine fishes that can safely be kept in such cramped quarters. Being inactive, peaceful fishes, they do not require much swimming space and seem to enjoy the company of other seahorses. More importantly, they live in shallow coastal areas where they must cope with regular inundations of fresh water from rivers, estuaries, and torrential rains. As a result, they have learned to adapt to a variety of conditions and can tolerate a wide range of salinities and temperatures providing the changes are not too rapid. For example, they can easily withstand a 10°F change in temperature as long as it occurs gradually over the course of the day. With regard to their ability to tolerate such fluctuations, seahorses are much hardier than most marine fishes. This is important because the smaller the aquarium, the faster are the changes in temperature, salinity, and pH.

For best results, seahorse stables should be no smaller than 15 gallons in volume. Many customized miniature reef tanks, like the one shown here, are well over 100 gallons.

For best results, however, I recommend that large seahorses be kept in aquariums of 15 gallons or bigger, while five- or ten-gallon tanks are probably best for dwarf seahorses. The reason for this is that the larger tanks give inexperienced aquarists a greater margin for error. Due to the larger volume of water they hold, bigger tanks are more resistant to pollution problems and rapid changes in temperature, salinity, and pH, and are therefore more forgiving of the beginner's inevitable mistakes.

To assure your seahorses of the best water possible, their stable must be equipped with an efficient filtration system. In aquariums of ten gallons and up, this can easily be accomplished by installing a good undergravel filter along with a small canister filter filled with the proper chemical filtration media. This system will provide the right combination of mechanical, biological, and chemical filtration necessary to maintain optimum water quality, and it will do it while producing strong aeration with gentle circulation—ideal conditions for the seahorse.

No matter what type of tank you select as your stable, it must be cleaned thoroughly before setting it up. Obtain a new cellulose sponge (which you will hereafter reserve for aquarium use only) and scrub out the tank using a little non-iodized salt and water to remove any potentially harmful residues. Rinse it well afterwards, and your corral will be ready for use. This step is especially important if the tank has been previously used as an aquarium.

The next step is to place the clean aquarium in a location that is well away from cold drafts (air conditioners, doors that open to the outside, or window fans) and heat sources (radiators, heating vents, space heaters, etc.). Choosing the proper location will protect your seahorses from rapid temperature changes.

Southern slender or spotted seahorse (*Hippocampus reidi*). Some main points to remember when setting up the corral are to place the tank away from cold drafts and heat sources and to include plenty of hitching posts.

Once you've found the perfect place for your corral, fill the tank about two-thirds full of water and install the undergravel filters. Immerse the undergravel filter plate and tilt it upward to release any air that might be trapped beneath it. Holding the filter plate flat against the bottom, tap it against the back of the tank to dislodge any tiny bubbles that remain, and attach the airlifts. Depending on the size of the aquarium, the undergravel filter may have one, two, or more plates, each with its own airlift or bubbler stem. (Motorized under- gravels are not recommended for use with seahorses, since the power-

# Equipment

heads generate too much turbulence for such feeble swimmers. The more conventional airlift units are more suitable for your stable.)

The filter plates should then be covered with two to three inches of fine gravel (grains up to one-eighth inch in diameter) that has been thoroughly rinsed in fresh water to remove impurities. A bed of this depth and size is fine enough to provide mechanical filtration as well as sufficient surface area to support an adequate population of denitrifying bacteria for biological filtration, and yet has large enough particles to keep from becoming impacted too quickly. Calcareous gravel such as dolomite, calcite, or crushed coral makes the best substrate since it will help to buffer the water and maintain the pH at the correct level. Be sure to add a handful or two of "dirty gravel" from an established marine aquarium to seed the substrate with beneficial bacteria.

After the undergravel filters and substrate are in place, connect the air pump to the airlifts using a two- or three-way set of gang valves and the necessary lengths of airline tubing. Top off the tank and adjust the valves to produce a vigorous stream of bubbles, using the elbow attachment to deflect the flow across the surface of the water. If you're using an artificial mix, add the proper amount of salt crystals according to instructions. The flow of water through the gravel will quickly dissolve the salt, and the tank should clear up completely overnight, or within a day or two at most.

In the meantime, you can hook up your canister filter. Your pet dealer can help you select a small unit with a flow rate that will not cause too much turbulence in your seahorse tank.

The filtration media you place in the canister filter is extremely important. For best results, it should include a top layer and bottom layer of special filter pads made by bonding hydrophilic polymers to a synthetic matrix. Don't let the scientific jargon fool you— that's just a fancy way of saying the pads are made from modern polymeric materials with special capabilities. In fact, because of their polymer-loading properties, these new pads are often referred to simply as poly-filters or poly-pads. Sandwiched between the top and bottom layers of poly-type pads, you should include a packet of special chemical purification medium, which comes prepackaged in polyester filter bags and is designed to remove ammonia and other nitrogenous waste products. Just ask your local dealer for poly-filter pads, and chemipure units or packs, and he'll know exactly what you mean. If he doesn't keep them in stock, have him order them for you. (No matter what kind of filtration media you choose, make sure it is designed for use in salt water).

The chemical filtration media described above provide enormous benefits for the aquarist, especially the novice. First of all, they prevent the deadly "new-tank syndrome" of rapidly rising ammonia and nitrite levels, while eliminating the need for a lengthy break-in period or cycling process during which beneficial denitrifying bacteria are established in the filter bed. Secondly, they will maintain a nitrogen cycle balance even if the bio-filter is overloaded or breaks down. In addition, they help prevent disease by maintaining optimum water quality even under adverse conditions. Finally, they simplify aquarium maintenance by reducing the need for frequent water changes.

The poly-type filter pads are able to do all this because they remove toxic metals and *excessive* amounts of ammonia, nitrite, nitrate, phosphates, and other dissolved organics *without* removing vital trace elements. What's more, they remove these excess waste products while still leaving an adequate amount of ammonia to sustain normal biological filtration. The chemi-pure units or packs work in much the same way to produce similar results.

Fill the canister filter with layers of poly-type pads and chemical purification packs as described. Install the filter according to the manufacturer's instructions, making sure the intake tube reaches all the way to the bottom of the tank and that the spray bar goes across the top of the aquarium. Seahorses do not like stagnant water, but neither can they fight strong currents. When you have the spray bar and undergravel return tubes adjusted so they produce a gentle rippling across the surface of the water, the circulation is just right.

The mechanical, biological, and chemical filtration provided by this system produces sparkling water of unbelievable clarity. In fact, the aquarium water will be all but invisible, so that, like a rose imbedded in crystal, your seahorses will seem suspended in space. They will actually appear to be gliding or floating through the air rather than swimming through the water.

Although even the tiniest canister filter will cause too much turbulence in an aquarium of less than ten gallons, there is no reason smaller setups have to do without chemical filtration. In smaller tanks, an inside box filter can be used to hold the sandwich of poly-type pads and chemical purification medium instead of a canister. If your setup is too small for even a box filter, then you can place a poly-filter pad directly over the undergravel filter instead. The poly-pad should completely cover the undergravel filter plate, so make a slit or cutout in the pad to fit snugly around the airlift tube, and then place the gravel on top of the poly-filter. The combination of an undergravel filter and

Your local pet shop will have all the necessary equipment to get you started in seahorses. **Left:** A variety of canister filters. **Right:** A box of saltwater sea mix.

a poly-type pad will furnish the smallest seahorse stable with efficient filtration.

Now that the filters are operating properly, you can decorate the aquarium, taking care to provide your stable with plenty of hitching posts. *Properly cured* rocks, branching coral, the blackened skeletons of sea fans and gorgonians, and plastic aquarium plants are all perfect for this. Pre-cured decorations purchased from a marine aquarium store are safest, since they will have been selected and prepared specifically for use in salt water.

However, the seahorse corral should not be too heavily decorated. Live foods will take full advantage of the many hiding places furnished by an overabundance of coral and rockwork, making it difficult for your seahorses to get enough to eat. This is especially dangerous when you're feeding freshwater foods, such as *Gammarus fasciatus*, daphnia, blackworms, or bloodworms, which don't last long in salt water. If they die in some isolated nook or cranny, they can foul the aquarium.

Consequently, when it comes to decorating your stable, I suggest something like the following arrangement. Slope the gravel so it is higher in the back of the tank than the front, shaping miniature sand dunes here and there to add interest. Select a choice piece of staghorn or finger coral for your centerpiece, and add one or two cured sea fans or gorgonians in a pleasing arrangement. If you prefer, you may substitute a few attractive, artificial marine plants in place of the sea fans or sea whips. As a finishing touch, you may want to include a nicely sculpted arch or spire of red organpipe coral, plus one or two colorful seashells, to complete the exhibit.

In addition, the seahorse stable should be topped with a tight-fitting cover glass and a fluorescent light fixture. A well-fitted cover will retard evaporation, keep potential contaminants out of the aquarium, and keep salt spray in the tank where it belongs. A fluorescent fixture with a light spectrum especially balanced to promote the growth of aquarium plants is equally important. Seahorses need plenty of light when feeding to track down their live foods, and bright light also helps to encourage the growth of green algae.

A lush growth of green algae is very beneficial in a marine aquarium because it releases oxygen into the water while removing dissolved carbon dioxide and nitrates. The lights should be left on for a minimum of 12–14 hours a day to get a good growth of algae started.

If you find the algae unsightly, I recommend allowing it to grow freely on the back of the aquarium while keeping the sides, the front, and the coral clear of algae. An algae scraper will keep the glass clean and the coral can be kept snowy white by dipping it in a dilute solution of muriatic or hydrochloric acid whenever the algae begins to build up on it. After the acid bath, the coral should be thoroughly rinsed in fresh water and allowed to dry in the sun before returning it to the aquarium.

Once your seahorse setup is fully operational, it will require only a little routine maintenance to keep it running smoothly. The undergravel filter should be operated constantly to provide continuous aeration and mechanical and biological filtration. The canister filter, on the other hand, must be turned off when the seahorses are fed. Otherwise it will filter out the brine shrimp, *Gammarus*, and other live foods before your pets have a chance to eat them. It is a good idea to unplug the canister filter when the seahorses are given their first feeding in the morning, and to plug it back in at night when they have finished feeding for the day.

Seahorses do fine in salt water with a specific gravity as low as 1.020 or as high as 1.025, with a salinity somewhere between these extremes being the best. This can easily be achieved by checking the specific gravity with a hydrometer when the aquarium is first set up. If the salinity is too low, add a little more artificial sea salt to raise it. If it is too high, add a little fresh water to lower the salinity.

Adjust the specific gravity in this manner until the hydrometer reads about 1.022–1.023, and mark the water level at that point on the outside of the tank using a grease pencil or tiny strip of adhesive tape. When evaporation drops the water level below this mark, add distilled water or aged, dechlorinated tap water to raise the water-line back to normal. The proper salinity can be maintained indefinitely using this simple procedure.

Provided that changes take place gradually, seahorses can tolerate a wide range of temperatures. However, they are susceptible to fungus and "ich" when chilled, so a small aquarium heater is a good investment for hobbyists in colder regions. Your local dealer can advise

A sprig of organpipe coral (*Tubipora* species).

you as to what wattage and type of heater is best for your size aquarium. Adjust the heater to maintain the temperature at around 78°–80°F (25–27°C), and you should have no problems.

To prevent detritus from accumulating in the filter bed and eventually clogging it, the gravel should be cleaned periodically. This is best done by stirring the top layer of the gravel to release trapped particles while siphoning off about 10% of the aquarium water on a monthly basis. To minimize the disruption of the bio-filter, however, it is important that no more than about one quarter of the gravel bed is cleaned in this way each month. Providing a different quarter of the substrate is washed each time, the entire filter bed will still be cleaned

Pet shops stock a variety of kits used to test the water chemistry of the tank. Such kits are extremely helpful to all aquarists—beginners and experts alike.

three times over the course of the year following this routine. The dirty water that is siphoned off should be replaced with new salt water that is approximately the same temperature and salinity as the aquarium water.

Do not discard the dirty water that is removed when cleaning the gravel. Instead, allow the impurities to settle out, drain off the clear salt water, and use it to raise brine shrimp. You will find that this recycled aquarium water produces excellent hatching rates.

As for the pH of the water, the seahorse fancier need not be overly concerned about acid water. The bed of calcareous gravel, chemical filtration, green algae, and partial water changes that occur when cleaning the gravel all serve to stabilize the pH nicely. It has been my experience that, given efficient filtration and proper aquarium management, the pH will usually take care of itself.

Besides cleaning a portion of the bed periodically, you will also have to replace the chemical filtration media as necessary. For example, each chemi-pure unit will filter up to 40 gallons for a period of six to eight months. In a seahorse stable of 20 gallons or less, they should be good for at least the full eight months. Color changes in the poly-type pads indicate when they need to be replaced. The poly-filters turn brown as they absorb dissolved organic wastes. When they turn black, indicating heavy organic loading, they should be changed. Like the chemi-pure units, the poly-pads should be good for several months before they have to be replaced.

I also highly recommend that the seahorse rancher keep an aquarium log in which to record important data. The entries should include weekly hydrometer readings, the dates when the gravel was "vacuumed" and the portion of water changed, when the chemical filtration media was changed, when the coral was last cleaned, and so forth. This information will be very useful in helping the aquarist stick to a routine maintenance schedule. In addition, be sure to note any other significant events, such as the addition of a new specimen (or the loss of an old one), courtship and breeding activity, the development of baby sea ponies, any disease problems, etc. This will encourage the hobbyist to make detailed daily observations of his seahorses and their stables—one of the secrets of successful aquarium keeping.

If you already have one or more marine aquariums, there is an easy way to add seahorses to your collection. Simply place a sheet of glass diagonally across an unobstructed corner of your community tank. This will form a triangular enclosure in which the seahorses may safely be kept, protected from more aggressive fishes that might otherwise harass them or gobble up all their food while the slower hippocampids go hungry. Seahorses don't need much swimming space, and they will usually be quite content in such an arrangement. For instance, if the sides of the triangle formed by the enclosure are 12 inches or more in length, it will comfortably house a pair of large seahorses. Of course, dwarf seahorses will live happily in a much smaller enclosure. Just be sure to give them a hitching post of some sort, and place their food directly in the triangular compartment with the seahorses.

If you would like to keep seahorses but you've never had an aquarium of any kind before, much less a saltwater setup, then I suggest you try the following sure-fire formula for success. Obtain a ten-gallon, all-glass container with a tightly fitting cover and a fluorescent light fixture. Set it up as previously described, installing an undergravel filter along with a *small* canister filter packed with poly-type filter pads and a chemi-pure unit. Run the filters continuously for two to three days while you prepare a battery of brine shrimp hatcheries. The brine shrimp eggs will hatch out in 24–48 hours, at which time you can safely stock the tank with several pygmy seahorses (*Hippocampus zosterae*). A dozen or so dwarves would make a good selection for starters.

With its efficient filtration and a carrying capacity that can easily support ten times as many dwarves, this setup gives the novice a huge margin for error. It is capable of absorbing all but the most disastrous mistakes he might possibly make. As long as the dwarf seahorses are healthy to begin with, they should thrive with no problems. With a little luck, they may even breed eventually. In that event, the ten-gallon tank is roomy enough to raise the entire brood along with their parents. There are no guarantees in the aquarium hobby, but this trouble-free setup is about as close to a sure thing as you can get.

Of course, no discussion of filtration systems for marine aquariums would be complete without mentioning the new miniature reef setups. The miniature reef filtration systems are well named, for they maintain water of such high quality and purity that even the most delicate invertebrates can thrive in it, making it possible to keep a living, growing reef in your home for the

# SEAHORSES IN THE MINIATURE REEF

first time. No longer must the aquarist content himself with the bleached bones and skeletal remains of coral and gorgonians. Now he can fill his tanks with the real thing—the living animals in all their glory. When it comes to filtration for small, closed-system aquariums, the miniature reef setups are state-of-the-art technology, and the ultimate goal of most serious aquarists today is to eventually have one of their own. Best of all, they are ideal setups for seahorses.

The miniature reef filtration systems, also known as dry/wet filters, achieve their spectacular results through a unique arrangement of special components. The separate components of these filters are available in many different designs, and there are endless variations in the way the components are combined, but in my opinion the miniature reef setups feature the following arrangement of components: (1) an overflow DLS pre-filter, (2) a dry filter for aerobic bio-filtration, (3) wet gravel chamber(s), and (4) a denitra filter for anaerobic bio-filtration.

The first component of such miniature reef systems is the pre-filter. This consists of a double layer spiral (DLS) module submerged in an overflow chamber attached to the side of the aquarium. (The DLS module contains the same modern polymeric material as the poly-type filter pads.) The primary purpose of the pre-filter is to provide mechanical filtration, removing all suspended particles from the water before it passes through the rest of the system. This it does with

**Facing page:** The miniature reef setup, resembling a vivid vegetarian platter, is the ideal habitat for seahorses. Note the purple gorgonians, yellow sea whips, and orange dendrophylliid coral.

remarkable efficiency thanks to its special design. The double layer of polymeric material is arranged in a spiral, which provides 6000cm$^2$ of surface area, giving the pre-filter an enormous holding capacity for dirt. In addition, the low resistance of this design prevents clogging so well that the pre-filter can normally be run for one or two *years* before it needs to be rinsed.

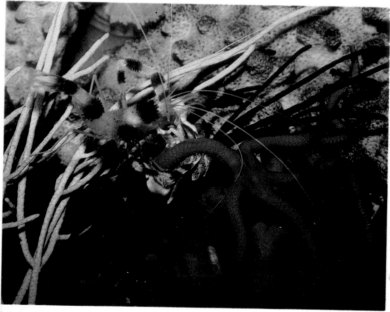

Banded coral shrimp and orange serpent starfish amid colorful sea whips and sponges.

The clean water from the pre-filter is then fed through a rotating sprinkler, allowing it to trickle through a second double layer spiral module with 40,000cm$^2$ of surface area. This is the "dry" filter component of the miniature reef setup, so called because the DLS module is not submerged in water. Rather, a very thin layer of water slowly trickles across the surface of the filter media to provide maximum air/water contact. The large surface area of this DLS module supports a tremendous population of aerobic, or oxygen-loving, bacteria (*Nitrosomonas* and *Nitrobacter*) for bio-filtration. The purpose of the dry filter is to furnish maximum aeration for high-capacity biological filtration, thereby reducing toxic ammonia to a relatively harmless nitrate while mineralizing other wastes. It is so ultra-efficient at doing this that an average 500-liter marine aquarium uses only about 1% of the dry filter's total capacity. With a reserve capacity of nearly 99%, it would be virtually impossible for the aquarist to accidentally overload the bio-filter and foul such a tank.

After leaving the dry filter, the water passes through one or more wet gravel chambers. These are simply extra-large beds of calcareous gravel, with a very high surface area, which serve to buffer the water and stabilize the pH.

The buffered water then passes through a special "denitra" filter. The denitra filter consists of double layer spiral modules equipped with special food bags that nourish a great mass of *anaerobic* bacteria. Although the nitrates and mineral wastes produced by the *aerobic* bacteria in the dry filter are relatively harmless, they can build up to unhealthy levels over a period of time. (Live corals and anemones are especially sensitive to high nitrate levels.) The anaerobic bacteria in the denitra filter are very effective at removing nitrates as well as preventing mineralization and the subsequent eutrophication, or over-fertilization, that might otherwise result.

Some miniature reef filtration systems also include a protein skimmer to help remove dissolved organic compounds such as albumin, phenols, organic acids, and chromophoric (color causing) compounds. The best of these units use an ozone generator in conjunction with the protein skimmer. The ozonizer increases the efficiency of the skimmer as well as killing bacteria and free-swimming parasites. This naturally helps prevent disease and promotes faster healing.

The end result of all this filtration is water of exceptional purity and clarity with rock solid pH. When it is finally returned to the aquarium, the water will have nearly zero levels of ammonia, nitrite, nitrate, and other waste products.

Beside state-of-the-art filtration, the second key to miniature reef setups is proper lighting. Ordinary fluorescent lights are not adequate to sustain the zooxanthellae, or symbiotic algae, that live in the tissues of corals and anemones, providing them with much of their nourishment.

To keep a living reef healthy requires a minimum of four full-length fluorescent lights with specially balanced spectrums. Some experts recommend halogen quartz iodide lamps for your miniature reef, used at the rate of three to five watts per gallon for at least 12–14 hours daily.

However, even with the best lighting and filtration possible, it still takes time to establish a coral jungle in your living room. Once the filter has been run in, the first step is to fill your tank with living rocks using about two pounds of live rock per gallon of aquarium capacity. These rocks will be heavily overgrown with slimy algae and bacteria, and the miniature reef is not a pretty sight at this point, for it looks exactly like what it is—a tank full of slimy rocks.

During this time, the water is filtered constantly and the unwanted algae is removed about once a week. After a couple of months of this, thick layers of filamentous green algae begin to cover the rocks. This is a healthy sign of improvement, although the hairy algae is still unsightly. Over the next few months, this filamentous algae is gradually replaced by attractive marine plants. Over 20 species of *Caulerpa* and dozens of kinds of red algae commonly appear in miniature reef tanks at this stage.

This is when the living rock really starts to live up to its name. As if by magic, thousands of minute creepy crawlers suddenly appear. Baby bristleworms and brittle stars, small snails and nudibranchs, and countless tiny crustaceans spring up out of nowhere.

For example, I remember the time an all but invisible speck on the aquarium glass caught my eye. As the days went by, I could see that it was a tiny mollusk of some kind. Before I knew it, my "mystery mollusk" had grown into a keyhole limpet the size of a quarter. Such surprises are everyday events in a miniature reef setup.

When this explosion of life occurs, and calcareous green algae such as *Halimeda* start to grow, the big moment has finally arrived. Delicate invertebrates can now be safely introduced to the aquarium. For starters, this includes stony corals of all sorts, with their pastel polyps of snowy white, pink, peach, and mint green. Then there are the soft corals and gorgonians: sea fans whose lacy structure gives them the appearance of living doilies, and sea whips with brilliant branches like painted pipe cleaners. Sea anemones provide the fragile flowers for this undersea garden, complete with poisonous petals. Sponges of all sizes, shapes, and colors nestle amid the coral like ornaments on the boughs of a Christmas tree. And don't forget the filter-feeding bivalves: flame scallops with their fiery beard of tentacles and tridacnid clams—miniature versions of the legendary man-eating clams—with emerald green mantles spangled with spots of bright blue and splashes of purple. Be sure to add several giant tube worms, which will unfurl their feathery crowns like so many gaily colored parasols. Slowly but surely, introducing one or two carefully selected specimens at a time, the aquarist creates a coral jungle of his own—a miniature reef of breathtaking natural beauty.

Flame scallop (*Lima scabra*) against a background of an organpipe coral skeleton.

Marine fishes can also be kept in a miniature reef setup, but they must be selected with the utmost caution. Obviously, fishes that feed on live coral, anemones, sponges, and algae must be strictly avoided. Unfortunately many of the most popular and desirable marine fishes fall into this category, including butterflyfishes, tangs or surgeonfishes, parrotfishes, and most angels. Other fishes must be excluded because they disrupt the miniature reef by burrowing or a tendency to rearrange the aquarium to their own liking. These include large wrasses, triggerfishes, and jawfishes.

On the other hand, seahorses are ideal inhabitants for this sort of setup. They will not disturb the miniature reef in any way, and the marine plants, sea fans, sea whips and gorgonians will provide them with natural hitching posts. I cannot imagine a more stunning display than several seahorses gliding majestically through one of these colorful undersea gardens with the gaudy gorgonians and fronds of *Caulerpa* swaying and rippling gently in the current. Best of all, many fishes feel so at home in the natural surroundings of a miniature reef that they spawn repeatedly: several gobies, clownfishes, and damsels as well as *large seahorses*. This is especially notable because the larger species of seahorses are often reluctant to breed in conventional tanks.

In short, the dry/wet miniature reef filtration systems are expensive and must be established patiently over a period of several months, while closely monitoring the nitrogenous wastes, but the results are truly spectacular. Once established, they are fairly easy to maintain, since they eliminate the need for regular partial water changes and washing the gravel. And, once again, they are perfect for seahorses.

27

# FEEDING YOUR SEAHORSES

Once their stable is ready, the aquarist must make arrangements to feed the herd of hungry horses that will soon be cavorting about in their new corral. When seahorses put on the ol' feed bag, it means one thing—live food and lots of it.

Keeping pygmy seahorses (*Hippocampus zosterae*) well fed is simple. Newly hatched brine shrimp (*Artemia salina*) are an ideal food for dwarves as well as the fry and juveniles of the larger species up to three to four inches in length. This food can easily be provided by incubating *Artemia* cysts (brine shrimp eggs) in special hatching containers. Many commercially made brine shrimp hatcheries are available, but the aquarist can easily set up one of his own using an inexpensive vibrator air pump, an airstone, and a quart mason jar. Attach the airstone to a length of airline tubing and connect the tubing to the air pump. Insert the airstone into the quart jar so that it reaches all the way to the bottom, and secure it in place by loosely stretching a rubber band around the mouth of the jar, taking care not to kink or crimp off the airline in so doing. Fill the jar two-thirds full of synthetic salt water or a special brine solution made by dissolving eight level tablespoons of non-iodized salt per gallon of water. Then add about one-quarter teaspoon of eggs to the jar, and adjust the airstone so it bubbles vigorously, keeping the eggs in suspension.

In 24–48 hours the eggs will begin to hatch. Before they can be fed to your seahorses, however, the nauplii (baby brine shrimp) must be separated from the indigestible egg shells. This can be done simply by turning off the air pump and allowing the water to settle for a few minutes, since the eggs will usually either float or sink. A flashlight can then be used to concentrate the nauplii in the center of the jar (brine shrimp are attracted to light). The concentrated brine shrimp can be harvested by sucking them up in a baster, placing a fine-

**Facing page:** Golden seahorse. A healthy seahorse is a well-fed seahorse. Seahorses seem to have bottomless pits; therefore, a constant food supply is essential.

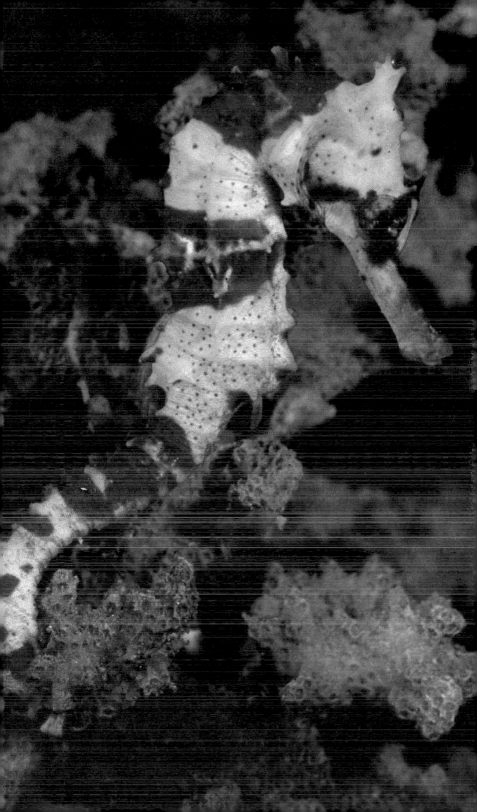

meshed brine shrimp net over the mouth of the jar, and straining the shrimp-laden water in the baster through the net so that it trickles back into the hatching container. More eggs can then be added to the quart jar, and the same brine solution can be used for a week or more of hatchings before it has to be replaced. (Once the sediment has settled out, the water removed from the aquarium while cleaning the gravel makes an excellent hatching solution.)

Depending on how many hungry seahorses you have to feed, a battery of two, three, or more hatching jars can be operated from the same air pump using a set of gang valves. You can then assure yourself of a steady supply of newly hatched brine shrimp at all times merely by alternating the jar from which you harvest the nauplii each day.

In addition, anyone within a reasonable distance of the ocean has an inexhaustible supply of food for dwarf seahorses at his very doorstep. This is marine plankton, a rich "soup" made up of countless tiny animals (zooplankton) and plants (phytoplankton), including larval crustaceans of all kinds. To collect this superb food, a plankton net (an elongated, conical net of fine material) is towed slowly through the water, and its contents are periodically emptied into a collecting container. After a collecting trip, the plankton laden water may then be strained through a brine shrimp net and the plankton residue deposited in the seahorse tank. Needless to say, if you are able to provide it, nutritious plankton is the perfect food for small seahorses of all kinds.

However, seahorses larger than three or four inches require more substantial food than plankton or baby brine shrimp. In their natural habitat, giant seahorses feed primarily on the tiny half-inch grass shrimp that live in the shallow weed beds. Grass shrimp is an all-purpose term that is loosely applied to several species of small marine shrimp as well as to the young of a variety of larger shrimp. This is the best food for large seahorses, and if you can possibly get it for them, they will prefer it to all others.

If you are among the 89 million Americans who now live within an hour's drive from the seashore, you will find that grass shrimp can be easily collected at low tide by vigorously shaking clumps of seaweed into a plastic bucket of sea water, or by dragging a small seine or large aquarium net through the grass flats. Tipping over stones and coral rocks at low tide is another productive technique that often reveals large quantities of grass shrimp and huge numbers of *Gammarus locusta*, a small hard-bodied shrimp that is commonly called the side-swimmer. Be sure to replace the rocks exactly as you

Close-up of a gorgonian showing its large polyps. These polyps are capable of eating small brine shrimp. However, this doesn't mean that you can overfeed your seahorses and rely on other marine creatures to clean up the leftovers. Always remember that several small meals are better than one that is too big, as excess food will foul the tank.

found them, and remember that seahorses swallow their food whole, so keep only those shrimp that are one-half-inch long or smaller.

Those of you who live too far from the sea to make regular trips can still supply your pet ponies with this superb natural food. All you have to do is plan a special expedition to the seashore well enough in advance so that you can spend an entire day, or weekend, collecting as many live shrimp as possible. The grass shrimp should then be quick-frozen in small plastic bags to preserve them until needed. With a little luck, you may be able to collect a year's supply of seahorse food in one trip this way. If you cannot manage to make such a trip personally, perhaps you know a friend or neighbor who could be persuaded to get them for you during his vacation.

At feeding time, place a small bag of frozen grass shrimp in a glass of water and, as soon as it melts, drop several of the thawed shrimp directly in front of your seahorses. They will nearly always eat their favorite food with relish, even after it has been frozen. This is the only non-living food that is acceptable to seahorses and nourishing enough to sustain them for a long period of time.

Aquarists who have a chance to visit the ocean only once in a great while may find it more convenient to culture *Gammarus lo-*

*custa* at home. The side-swimmers can be kept in a flat glass pan, a plastic shoe box, or any similar shallow container that has been filled with salt water and furnished with a *thin* layer of fine sand on the bottom. Place the culture container where it will get plenty of sun, and add several pieces of algae-covered coral rubble or shells. The *Gammarus* will gather under the coral and shells, clinging to them for protection. It is then a simple matter to place a piece of rubble or two in

Moored safely in place, seahorses spend most of the day resting and waiting for prey to pass within reach. A hunting seahorse will often stretch out horizontally to extend its range, as the swarthy stallion is doing here.

the aquarium at feeding time. Once the seahorses have picked them clean, the coral rocks and shells can be returned to the culture container. Whenever possible, restock the culture with freshly collected *Gammarus* to keep it going strong. The culture can be maintained indefinitely in this manner as long as the feedings do not deplete the side-swimmers faster than their rate of reproduction can increase their population.

Without easy access to these natural foods, the inland aquarist is faced with a far greater challenge when it comes to feeding giant

# Feeding Your Seahorses

seahorses. In order to give them as varied a diet as possible, he is forced to rely on foods such as adult brine shrimp, freshwater *Gammarus fasciatus*, mosquito larvae, bloodworms, daphnia, blackworms, and live baby guppies or mollies. To assure a steady supply of these foods, the landlocked hobbyist will most likely have to raise them himself.

For example, brine shrimp can be raised to maturity in an aquarium of 20 gallons or larger filled with artificial salt water at a salinity of 1.020. The tank should be aerated heavily and kept in a location where it receives bright sunlight to encourage the growth of algae. Add one-half teaspoon of brine shrimp eggs and, after 48 hours, feed the emerging nauplii *sparingly* by sprinkling a pinch of dry baker's yeast on the surface of the water along with a bit of finely ground baby fish food. This will cloud the water, which will gradually begin to clear as the baby brine shrimp develop. Each feeding should cloud the water for only two or three days at the most, and the brine shrimp should *not* be fed again until the water is crystal clear. The first generation of *Artemia* will reach maturity in about three weeks, and the culture will then be self-sustaining.

However, unlike grass shrimp and *Gammarus*, adult brine shrimp are not an adequate diet for large seahorses. Under ideal conditions, giant seahorses may live a year or more on a steady diet of adult brine shrimp, but the average aquarist is apt to find that their life span is considerably shortened if they are fed *Artemia salina* alone. Evidently there are not enough vitamins and minerals—especially calcium—in the soft-bodied brine shrimp to keep large seahorses healthy for long. The inland aquarist must therefore supplement their diet with other live foods.

Fortunately, freshwater *Gammarus fasciatus* are perfect for this, since these hard-bodied crustaceans are substantial enough to serve as the staple food for large seahorses. *Gammarus fasciatus* can be collected from the vegetation and leaves littering the bottoms of ponds and streams, and like its marine relative, it can easily be cultured in a spare tank, plastic wading pool, or similar receptacle. Use an airstone in one corner of the tank, and feed them sparingly with chopped raw spinach and a pinch of dry fish food. A heavy growth of algae is very beneficial, and they should be kept in slightly alkaline water of medium hardness with a temperature of 74°–78°F (23–26°C). At this temperature, an average of 22 eggs will be produced every 11 days throughout the year. To feed these quarter-inch crustaceans to your fish, siphon out the desired amount of them, straining the water through a net, and dump the contents of the net into your aquarium.

Like *Gammarus fasciatus*, bloodworms will survive in salt water long enough to be useful as food for giant seahorses. Bloodworms, which are actually the larvae of midges (*Chironomus*), are difficult to collect in quantity because they spend much of their time buried in the bottom mud, but they are sometimes available from fish dealers—especially in the fall and winter. It is a good idea to buy all the live bloodworms you can get when they are in season, since the bright red quarter- to half-inch long larvae can be stored indefinitely by placing them in shallow trays kept in a lighted refrigerator set at about 40°F. Under these conditions, the larvae will neither pupate nor eat, remaining in a kind of suspended animation until needed. At temperatures above 55°F, the larvae may pupate, while temperatures below 32°F may kill them.

Live blackworms and tubifex worms are also sometimes available from aquarium stores. Like bloodworms, the blackworms are also acceptable food for large seahorses, but the aquarist should avoid feeding them tubifex worms. Tubifex die very quickly in salt water and are thus much more likely to serve as a source of pollution than a source of food for your seahorses.

Another live food the inland aquarist can use to round out the diet of his seahorses is mosquito larvae. Although they are seldom available from dealers, they are very easy to raise. All you need to do is get a big plastic bucket or washtub, fill it with water, and set it outside in the shade. The female mosquitos in your neighborhood will be only too happy to lay their eggs on the surface in rafts of 100–300 measuring about one-eighth inch across. The larvae, or "wrigglers" as they are known for obvious reasons, hang at the surface to breathe and filter the water for food. You can hasten their development by tossing a few handfuls of leaves or a little rabbit chow into the tub to promote the growth of bacteria on which the wrigglers feed.

Depending on the temperature, the life cycle from egg to flying adult takes from six days to over two weeks. Therefore, if you harvest the larvae regularly, you can prevent any of the wrigglers from maturing into pesky adults. To harvest the larvae, simply strain the water through a fish net.

When cold weather approaches, you should begin collecting the egg rafts to store in your refrigerator (once refrigerated, the eggs can be hatched out up to 12 years later!). The eggs can then be hatched out as needed to provide your seahorses with mosquito larvae throughout the winter.

In addition, live baby guppies and mollies are also excellent seahorse foods. Mollies are the best for this since they can be con-

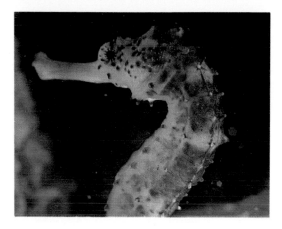

Indian Ocean seahorses feeding on a swarm of brine shrimp, the floating white specks. Brine shrimp is a staple that can be raised at home.

verted to live in salt water by using a good brand of synthetic sea salt to slowly raise the salinity of their aquarium over a period of a few weeks. The obviously pregnant mollies can then be transferred to a breeding trap *directly* in the seahorses' tank where their fry will survive until they are eaten.

I strongly recommend that the inland aquarist maintain a culture of *Gammarus*, adult brine shrimp, mosquito larvae, and/or a tank of breeding mollies at all times to help keep up with his seahorses' voracious appetites. A large seahorse can easily eat 75–125 adult brine shrimp or *Gammarus* daily, and even a two-week old pony will eat as many as 3000–4000 baby brine shrimp a day. In view of this, collecting enough *Gammarus*, mosquito larvae, and daphnia from ponds and streams to satisfy your seahorses would be difficult if not impossible, making live food cultures a necessity. If you must limit yourself to one kind of culture, *Gammarus fasciatus* is probably the best, since it is readily eaten, lasts well in salt water, and is very nourishing.

In fact, adult brine shrimp and *Gammarus* are the only live foods that you can be certain your large seahorse will eat. Bloodworms, mosquito larvae, and baby guppies are simply too big for medium-sized seahorses (three to four inches) to take, and many larger seahorses are also reluctant to eat these "unnatural" substitutes. Like everything else, the food preferences and eating habits of seahorses vary from individual to individual. So before you commit yourself to raising a particular type of live food, be sure to offer it to your seahorse on several occasions to make sure your pet pony will accept his new fodder.

Some large seahorses can be trained to accept frozen brine shrimp that has been carefully thawed and swirled through the water in a lifelike manner. This is an unreliable method of feeding at best because, unlike frozen grass shrimp, seahorses eventually lose interest in frozen *Artemia* and will usually refuse to eat it after a few weeks. However, it *can* be a real lifesaver in an emergency. Should your culture(s) fail, or if a seashore collecting trip should prove to be unproductive, frozen brine shrimp can keep your seahorses alive until better foods are available. In a pinch, it can also be used to stretch your live food cultures when they become depleted.

Considering their bottomless stomachs, the landlocked hobbyist would be well advised to limit himself to a pair of giants rather than keeping a whole herd of hungry horses. In fact, if the inland aquarist is not prepared to maintain live food cultures, he should stock his stables with the easy-to-feed dwarf seahorses.

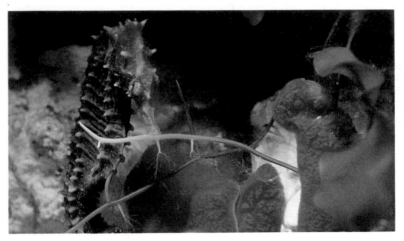

When a seahorse is really hungry, it will actively seek out food. When given too much of a good thing, the stallion may reconnoiter and even kill prey that it has no intention of eating.

No matter what you feed them, it is important to remember that several smaller feedings a day are much better than one big daily feeding. The reason for this is that seahorses require a constant, adequate but *not excessive*, supply of food in order to thrive. They feed continuously through most of the daylight hours, so some food should be present at all times or they can become malnourished. However, if too much live food is offered at one time, once they have eaten all they can hold, seahorses will often continue to attack and kill their prey without swallowing it. It seems that when some tasty tidbit passes by within easy reach, seahorses simply cannot resist the urge to attack it, even though they are not the least bit hungry.

When this happens, the seahorse will greedily slurp up its prey in the usual manner, only to spit it out again immediately after-

# Feeding Your Seahorses

wards, rather worse for wear. I have seen a seahorse inhale and reject its crippled victim in this way several times in rapid succession, until its mangled prey stopped moving. Not only is this wasteful, it's a source of potential pollution. The best way to keep your seahorses well fed while avoiding this sort of needless waste is by providing them with several small meals spread out over the course of the day.

In addition, when you're dealing with freshwater foods, which will perish sooner or later in salt water, small feedings are the only way to go. Serving modest portions will give your seahorses a chance to clean up such freshwater morsels before they die and foul the aquarium.

It is equally important to keep the seahorse corral well lighted. Brine shrimp, gammarids, and other live foods prefer to hug the bottom, and they blend in with the gravel very well, so your seahorses need plenty of light to search them out.

Feeding seahorses are fascinating to watch. Their preferred hunting technique is the ambush, patiently lying in wait with their tails securely anchored around some convenient hitching post. All the while, their independent eyes are keeping a sharp lookout for potential prey, one eye scanning upward while the other eye looks downward, so as not to miss anything passing nearby.

When some unsuspecting victim does blunder within striking distance, it's all over in a hurry. Drawing a bead on its dinner exactly as if its hollow snout were the barrel of a rifle, the seahorse gives a quick jerk of its head, accompanied by a distinctly audible "click," and its hapless victim is sucked up faster than the eye can follow. If you have ever collected fishes using a slurpgun, you will understand perfectly how a feeding seahorse accomplishes this vanishing act. The toothless jaws at the end of its snout operate with a rapid, spring-like action which produces a powerful suction that pulls its prey irresistibly, along with a little water. One moment its prey is there, and the next it's gone.

When seahorses are really hungry, however, they are not content to wait for their supper to come to them. If some mouth-watering morsel wanders by beyond their reach, they will take off in hot pursuit, often using their tails to push themselves along for added propulsion. Once they close the gap to within a quarter inch of their prey, that distinctive "snick!" will announce their victim's sudden demise. Or they may actively stalk their prey, skimming along just above the bottom, carefully searching every nook and cranny as they go. When you see your seahorses conducting these search-and-destroy missions, it's time to feed them.

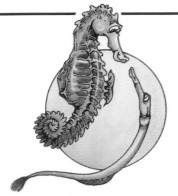

**N**ow that you've gotten the perfect seahorse setup running, and your live food production line has shifted into high gear, you will be anxious to stock your stable with thoroughbreds. No problem. Virtually all aquarium stores that handle marines make it a point to keep seahorses in stock, or will be able to order them for you without delay.

# STOCKING THE STABLE

## SEAHORSES AND GOOD PARDNERS

Your only worry will be to select prime specimens in the best of health that will thrive in the home you've carefully prepared for them.

In this chapter, I will show you how to tell the winners from the also-rans, so you can be sure you're bringing home a champion stallion and not some broken-down nag.

When picking out a seahorse, the first things to look for are obvious signs of disease such as tattered fins, fungus, or external parasites. For instance, seahorses that have been collected in trawls, or housed with fin-nipping fishes, often suffer severe fin damage as a result. This condition is not serious, since even seahorses whose fins have been nipped, eaten, or torn away entirely will usually regrow them completely within a few weeks. However, there is always a possibility that the fin damage may be due to fin rot, or that secondary infections may develop at a later date, so it's best not to take a chance on seahorses with ragged, limp fins.

Needless to say, seahorses with fungus should also be avoided. This problem is most common in late fall and winter, since seahorses that have been chilled often develop badly fungused areas on their bodies. Of course, localized fungus can occur at any time of year as the result of an injury. It will appear as a fuzzy, cotton-like growth at the site of the wound. It's a good idea to leave such specimens in the dealer's tank rather than attempting to treat them at home.

In addition, be sure to examine your potential pets for external parasites. Freshly collected seahorses are frequently infested with a nasty parasite known as the sea louse (*Argulus* sp.). These small, flat creatures assume the same coloration as their hosts, but careful observation will quickly reveal their presence. The favorite hiding place of these pests is around the seahorse's head, especially the nape of its

A pair of seahorses (*Hippocampus erectus*) tied to the hitching post. It goes without saying that only healthy specimens should be considered for life on the ranch.

neck, so be sure to check these areas closely. They will appear as small, semi-transparent bumps varying from pinpoint-sized babies to quarter-inch adults. Although these parasites are easily removed once discovered, heavily infested seahorses can become badly weakened from loss of blood. Seahorses that attempt to scratch themselves against the coral or gravel should likewise be rejected, since they are probably infected with a different kind of parasite.

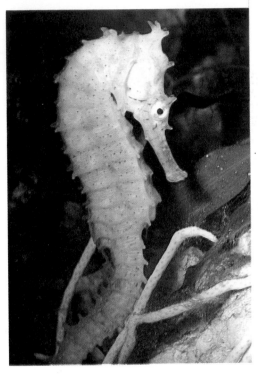

Note the tiny red dots on this pinto. These are part of this seahorse's natural coloration. If you have any doubts about the state of a particular horse's hide, don't buy it.

Once you have eliminated those specimens with obvious signs of disease, you must beware of one other thing. Seahorses have ravenous appetites and feed more or less continuously throughout the day. Therefore, if they have spent a long time in the collector's holding tanks, followed by an indefinite period at a wholesaler, they may become malnourished by the time they finally arrive at your local pet store. To check for this, observe the seahorse head-on: the body of a well-fed seahorse should be slightly rounded or convex in cross-section, while a malnourished specimen will have a concave appearance.

# Stocking the Stable

A seahorse that is clearly gaunt and emaciated should be passed over. If possible, try to obtain freshly collected specimens at the peak of their stamina.

Now that you've narrowed your choices down to well-fed, seemingly healthy individuals, there is one final test your seahorses must pass before you bring them home. Ask the dealer to feed them. Seahorses are natural born gluttons. Ordinarily, they are *always* hungry. So if one of them shows no interest in live food, there is something seriously wrong with it. If the dealer keeps seahorses in stock, but does not have live food, such as adult brine shrimp, bloodworms, or blackworms on hand to feed them, it would be wise to purchase your horses somewhere else, since they will not have been fed properly while they were in his care. The seahorses you take home should be alert, have healthy appetites, and an active interest in food.

Now that you know how to tell the winners from the also-rans when you are looking over a tank full of seahorses, there are a number of species to choose from. Some of the more easily kept and readily available varieties are described below.

For instance, European aquarists can choose from two popular species that all reach a length of around seven to eight inches as adults. To begin with, take the short-snouted seahorse (*Hippocampus hippocampus*), a relatively undemanding species from the eastern Atlantic and Mediterranean. It is a favorite of European hobbyists because it assumes an attractive red coloration when kept under the right conditions. By contrast, a yellow-green coloration is typical of the Mediterranean seahorse (*Hippocampus ramulosus*).

On the other side of the Atlantic, we have the northern giant (*H. oroctus*), which grows to about eight inches. This seahorse was once common in the brackish portions of the Hudson River. It is usually black or dark brown in color with a highly variable pattern of white spots or blotches, giving it a somewhat mottled appearance. The southern slender or spotted seahorse (*H. reidi*) is very similar to its northern relative except that it prefers the warmer waters of Florida and the Caribbean. It is also very variable in coloration, typically with a brownish or blackish background color interspersed with lighter spots and patches.

Both the northern and southern giants are known for the unusually vivid color phases they sometimes exhibit. Nearly pure white or jet black specimens are not uncommon, and individuals that are buttercup yellow, flaming orange, or fire engine red are occasionally found. As you can imagine, these brilliantly colored specimens are much in demand.

The Hawaiian or golden seahorse (*Hippocampus kuda*) is a wide-ranging seahorse found throughout the western Pacific, Hawaii, and the Indian Ocean. It is often found in the open ocean drifting with the currents, which no doubt accounts for its wide distribution. Its normal coloration is a bright golden yellow with a few irregular darker markings, but when subjected to stress, it becomes peppered with black speckles, giving it an olive cast. When first transferred to your aquarium, it will remain in its stressed color phase. Give it a few weeks to settle down, and it will gradually assume its normal golden color as it gets used to new surroundings. *H. kuda* is said to reach a length of one foot in some parts of its range, but it is more commonly found at a size of about four inches.

If the amount of space or money you can devote to seahorses is strictly limited, or if you will have difficulty providing them with an adequate supply of live food for any reason, then the dwarf seahorse (*Hippocampus zosterae*) is the perfect choice for you. It is very inexpensive, very hardy, lives entirely on newly-hatched brine shrimp, and is easy to breed and raise throughout its two-year life span. *Hippocampus zosterae* is the Shetland pony of seahorses, reaching an adult size of about two inches. At this size, they can be housed comfortably in a two- to five-gallon aquarium, or even a large goldfish bowl, providing it is equipped with adequate filtration and aeration. Found primarily along the Gulf coast of Florida, they exhibit a variety

Swimming baby horseshoe crab (*Limulus polyphemus*), a helpful bottom scavenger.

Atlantic deer cowry (*Cypraea cervus*) alongside a featherduster worm.

of color phases from green to gold, yellow, brown, black, and white. In all respects save their size, they are identical to the larger species of *Hippocampus*. If you have never kept marine fishes before, maintaining a small tank of dwarves is the ideal way to start.

Regarding stablemates for your seahorses, companions for them must be chosen very carefully. Seahorses simply cannot compete in the same aquarium with faster, more aggressive fishes. Territorial fishes that are chronic chasers or fin-nippers will constantly harass seahorses, and greedily gobble up all of your precious live food before your slowpoke sea ponies can eat it.

Some other fishes must be ruled out because they might regard seahorses as their natural prey: for example sargassumfish (*Histrio histrio*), large groupers, and sea basses. Large sea anemones with powerful stings, such as tube anemones (*Cerianthus*) and carpet anemones, are also a threat to seahorses. Being weak swimmers, seahorses are unable to free themselves when they brush against nematocysts, and they are quickly overwhelmed as more and more tentacles wrap around them.

If you are interested in breeding seahorses, I strongly recommend that you keep them strictly by themselves. Even the smallest, most inoffensive specimens—that otherwise get along splendidly with seahorses—can wreak havoc among their newborn young. For example, I will never forget the trouble I had when a dwarf seahorse gave

Your aquarium dealer will be able to help you select compatible corals, sponges, and other tankmates for your seahorse stable.

birth in a community tank of carefully selected stablemates. The babies popped out of their father's pouch one or two at a time—perfect miniatures of their parents. Before long, the sea fan on which the pregnant male had settled was studded with dozens of tiny sea ponies, all hanging on tightly with their prehensile tails. The banded coral shrimp climbing up the sea fan seemed innocent enough, until I noticed it was systematically clearing a swath of baby sea ponies as it went. A closer look revealed that the candy-cane crustacean was popping the babies into its mouth as fast as it could—two at a time—without even breaking stride! I rescued the rest of the babies as soon as I realized what was happening, corralling them in a guppy breeding tank made of fine mesh netting, which I floated in one corner of the tank. Even safely inside the breeding trap, however, the little seahorses continued to disappear at an alarming rate. Each night I would count them before I went to bed, and all would seem well, yet each morning two or three more would be gone without a trace. I couldn't imagine what was happening to them until I finally caught the culprit in the act. A tiny starfish no bigger across than a nickel was preying on the baby seahorses as it crawled along the outside of the netting. When it came to one of the ponies anchored to the netting, it would pin down the tiny tail curled around the mesh, evert its stomach, and digest the hapless baby at its leisure—right through the netting!

Having learned my lesson the hard way, I now make it a point to give breeding seahorses a "paternity ward" of their own. Even when their tankmates pose no actual threat to the babies, they can still cause problems. Each of the fry can eat about 3500 newly hatched brine shrimp a day, so you'll need all the help you can get just to keep up with their appetites, without worrying about feeding any pipefish, gobies, or feather dusters that are living in the same tank.

Now that you've handpicked a selection of healthy seahorses and peaceful pard'ners, they must be carefully introduced to their new stable when you bring them home. *Do not open the bags and pour the specimens directly into the aquarium.* Instead, begin a gradual transition by floating the bags in your corral to equalize temperatures. After 15–30 minutes, add a little aquarium water to the bag water, watching your specimens closely for any signs of apparent distress. If they act normally and appear to be breathing properly, continue to add small portions of water at about ten-minute intervals. If the new arrivals are still behaving normally when the volume of water in their bags has been doubled, they can be gently released into the aquarium.

This slow mixing of the water will prevent lethal osmotic imbalances and shock from sudden pH and gas saturation changes. Gradually acclimating your seahorses is especially important when you are transferring them from natural sea water to artificial salt water.

As a reward for your diligence, you can now sit back and relax while your pets happily make themselves at home. You should have live food available at this time, since seahorses will often begin feeding moments after they are introduced to their corral. Few things are more gratifying than watching your new ponies contentedly stalking their prey as if they had never left the ocean.

Headstudy of Gray's pipefish (*Halicampus grayi*).

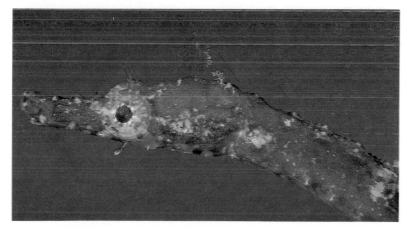

**O**nce your seahorses have happily set up housekeeping in their new home, and you've settled into a comfortable routine of feeding and maintenance, you may begin thinking about breeding your new pets. If you are keeping dwarf seahorses (*Hippocampus zosterae*), your chances for success are excellent. These pygmy ponies reproduce quite readily in captivity. Indeed, breeding is pretty much inevitable any time a number of them are kept together under favorable conditions. Although their normal breeding season is spring and summer in the wild, when they are well-fed and provided with green plants (*Halimeda*, *Penicillus capitatus*, *Caulerpa crassifolia*, etc.) to simulate their natural habitat, captive dwarf seahorses often breed year round.

# BREEDING AND RAISING

Surprisingly, several authors have reported that seahorses emit a repetitive drumming sound during the spawning season, and it is felt by some that this "mating call" serves to bring breeding individuals together in the vastness of the sea. But simply bringing a receptive male and female together is not enough, for seahorses select their mates carefully, following an elaborate courtship ritual.

With the dwarves, it is usually the male who breaks the ice. He will woo his lady by perching alongside her and vibrating his dorsal fin rapidly until his entire body begins to quiver and shake. If she is carrying eggs, the female will remain beside her beau and allow him to get fresh with her. Her paramour will then proceed to nudge her, wrap his tail about her, and generally manhandle his mate as if attempting to arouse her. Needless to say, the pygmy stallion will be very excited by this time, although his lady will often continue to calmly eat brine shrimp throughout this phase of their courtship!

Eventually, however, she will respond to his advances by extending her egg tube slightly. The pair will then push up from the plants and meet briefly in mid-water during the actual transfer of the eggs. The male will approach his mate with his pouch fully extended, she will insert her egg tube, and they will hang together in mid-water for ten to thirty seconds while her eggs surge downward deep into the male's pouch. Their mating accomplished, the exhausted lovers will then separate and settle down to rest. You almost expect to see them

A "loaded" male seahorse (*Hippocampus erectus*).

This head-down position is typical for a male that is about to deliver its young in 30 minutes to an hour. At this time, the brood pouch is beginning to open.

light up cigarettes at this point. Unfortunately, most seahorse breeders miss this magical moment because, when dwarves mate, it's all over in a matter of minutes.

After mating, the pygmy seahorse (*Hippocampus zosterae*) incubates its eggs for a period of around ten days. The male certainly feels the stirring of the young within his pouch, for he experiences definite labor pains as the gestation period nears the end. Often a male with a heavily bloated pouch will swim slowly to and fro in obvious discomfort. Or he may show his distress by twisting and turning while anchored in one spot, almost as if he were writhing in agony, while powerful spasms wrack his body. As these muscular contractions increase in frequency and regularity, the tightly closed pouch aperture begins to gape open. If you look closely, you can actually see a tangled mass of tiny eyes, heads, and tails within the pouch at this time.

The rhythmic contractions continue until, with a sudden spasmodic squeeze, a baby seahorse pops out. Expelling the young in this manner is hard work, and the exhausted male must take frequent rests from his exertions to recover. Consequently it may take several hours, or even a day or more, for the entire brood to be delivered. Occasionally, a pregnant male seems to have difficulty ejecting the last of its young. When this happens, he may have to forcibly scrape or rub

# Breeding and Raising

his pouch against the coral or bottom in order to dislodge them. Pygmy seahorses may give birth to as few as ten or as many as 70 babies at one delivery.

The young are usually born one at a time, although two or three sometimes pop out at once. They may emerge headfirst or tail-first, but once born, the baby seahorse is strictly on its own. For a few seconds after it is ejected, the newborn sinks helplessly, wriggling like a worm. All at once, it will straighten up, try out its fins and glide expertly over to the nearest hitching post. From that moment on, the pygmy pony is entirely capable of caring for itself. With the exception of its pug nose and bulging, oversized eyes, it is a miniature version of the adults.

Raising dwarf seahorses (*Hippocampus zosterae*) is easy. Providing your stable is large enough, the babies can be safely left in the same tank with their parents. From the moment they are born, they can be fed newly hatched brine shrimp. It is important that the brine shrimp be freshly hatched, however, since nauplii that are more than a day old are too big for the babies to swallow.

A good way to make sure that the newborns have an ample supply of the right size food at all times is by hatching brine shrimp directly in their nursery tank. Just sprinkle a pinch of the eggs on the surface of the aquarium water and they will hatch out in two days. Eggs from the San Francisco Bay area are best for baby seahorses, since the nauplii that hatch from them are slightly smaller than those from the Great Salt Lake. To prevent potential pollution problems, the unhatched eggs and empty eggshells should be removed from the nursery tank after a week or two by scooping them up in a fine daphnia net. (Of course, living microplankton is an even better food if you can provide it.)

Since the babies eat the same food as the adult dwarves, all that is really necessary to raise their young is to increase the food supply accordingly. This may require the purchase of an additional air pump to aerate a fresh battery of hatching jars, however, since you may be dealing with several dozen hungry fry, each of which can eat thousands of baby brine shrimp daily.

When the young are fed properly they grow at an amazing rate. Before you know it, they will be ready to mate and have babies of their own. It is not unusual for an aquarist to breed and raise successive generations of dwarf seahorses (*Hippocampus zosterae*) in captivity.

In fact, this is one species I can unhesitatingly recommend for the beginning marine aquarist. Not only can the beginner expect to keep his pygmies alive and healthy, he can look forward to breeding and raising them without too much expense or difficulty. With respect to their hardiness and ease of breeding, the dwarf seahorse can be considered the guppy of marine fishes.

When it comes to breeding and raising the larger species of seahorses, though, the picture is not so rosy. For some reason, they do not pair up and reproduce readily in the aquarium.

This is surprising, since their courtship and mating habits are the same as the dwarves', only on a grander scale. For example, with giant seahorses, it is often the female who makes the first move. However, just any old stallion won't do, and the selection process usually begins with the filly displaying before the eligible bachelor of her choice. She signals her interest by swimming "seductively" back and forth in front of, behind, and all around her prospective mate. If the male is receptive, he will quickly respond to her advances, gliding toward her at a full gallop. If all goes well, the female will respond with equal ardor, and the happy couple will then engage in a whirlwind courtship.

Anyone lucky enough to witness the charming courtship ritual that follows will never forget the sight. Once a compatible pair has formed, they clasp tails, looking for all the world like a young couple shyly holding hands. With their tails intertwined, they sway gracefully from side to side together until one of them begins to shudder with passion. It looks almost as if waves of pleasure are sending shivers down its spine, for the seahorse's entire body quivers with a rippling motion that would put a hula dancer to shame. As suddenly as they began, these amazing gyrations come to a complete halt, only to be resumed by the seahorse's partner. While one seahorse performs this rippling mating dance, its mate watches motionlessly as if rapt with sheer adoration. When one dancer stops, its partner quickly picks up the rhythm. Back and forth, this passionate *pas de deux* may go on for as long as half an hour in the larger species of seahorses.

When this fascinating mating dance finally comes to an end, the actual nuptials begin. This is the final phase of courtship. It is marked by an extremely awkward embrace intended to bring the female's ovipositor, or egg tube, into position to transfer her eggs into the male's pouch. More often than not, many difficult and delicate maneuvers—which sometimes end up with the seahorses inverted in relation to each other—are required before this is accomplished. Eventually, with the active cooperation of the male, the female succeeds in inserting her ovipositor into the opening at the top of his brood pouch, and begins depositing her eggs. Sometimes the male's elastic brood pouch

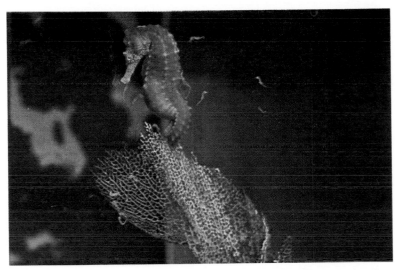

Male seahorse "in labor." Large seahorses deliver groups of young at a time, while dwarf ponies are usually born individually.

is filled to capacity on the first try, but often the nuptial embrace must be repeated several times before the pouch is full. Afterwards the male may go through a series of agitated contortions, twisting and stretching as though trying to rearrange the eggs more comfortably.

Seahorses do not believe in putting all their eggs in one basket, so to speak. When her partner's pouch contains all the eggs it can hold, the female immediately begins searching for another suitable male with which to mate. On the other hand, if she has already deposited the bulk of her eggs elsewhere, she may not have enough left to fill the male's pouch. In that case, the male may mate with a second or even a third female before it has all the eggs it can carry.

Either way, it's strictly "love 'em and leave 'em" as far as the female seahorse is concerned. The sex life of these fickle fillies consists of a series of one night stands. The moment a female deposits all of her eggs, she departs without so much as a backward glance, leaving the male literally "holding the bag."

At any rate, the moment the last egg is nestled safely inside, the slot-like opening at the top of the brood pouch seals itself. The eggs are fertilized, and placenta-like changes in the lining of the pouch begin immediately. Spongelike, its tissue expands as the capillaries and blood vessels that supply it swell and multiply. A film of tissue then forms around each, providing it with a compartment of its own. Thus, the pouch enfolds, protects, and nourishes the developing eggs.

It's a shame more aquarists don't have a chance to see the giant seahorse's spectacular mating ritual. The reasons they do not breed as freely in captivity as the dwarves are unclear. I suspect it may be due to the fact that it's more difficult to provide large seahorses with "natural" conditions and an adequate diet, and to give them a suitable selection of prospective mates from which to choose. Pygmy ponies are more at home in the cramped quarters of an aquarium, and they are often kept in herds, giving them an ample selection of potential partners. Giant seahorses *do* breed well in miniature reef setups, however. Perhaps this is because of the larger size of the miniature reefs, which are usually a minimum of 40 gallons. Or maybe it's due to the miniature reef's unsurpassed water quality and more natural surroundings, with its lush growth of marine plants and gorgonians.

Despite their reluctance to breed in a conventional setup, it is not at all unusual for large seahorses to give birth in the aquarium. This is because "loaded" or pregnant males are widely available in the spring (U.S. species mate in late winter). However, even when such

A pair of Mediterranean seahorses (*Hippocampus ramulosus*). Unfortunately, most aquarists have little or no luck in breeding large seahorses at home.

# Breeding and Raising

males obligingly produce a tank full of young, their fry have proven to be much more difficult to raise than those of the dwarf seahorse.

Why this should be is a mystery. The fry of the larger species are very similar in size and appearance to those of *Hippocampus zosterae*. Their eggs develop in precisely the same manner, each one safely enclosed in its own compartment formed by the placenta-like tissue lining the pouch. After an incubation period of 45–50 days, the males endure the same sort of "labor pains" as the pygmies, and deliver their young in the same way—forcibly ejecting them from the pouch. In the case of the giants, however, the babies are expelled in bunches, with as few as 10–15 or as many as 25–30 spewing out at a time. These mass expulsions usually take place over a period of several days, until a total of about 200–300 young have been delivered. The size of the brood varies with the size of the parent, and an exceptionally large male can deliver up to 600 fry at one time. The newborns are about one-quarter inch long, and are fully capable of eating newly hatched brine shrimp from the moment of birth.

Despite this, the infant mortality rate of large seahorses is typically very high, and it's not uncommon for the aquarist to lose an entire spawn. Perhaps the difficulty lies in the sheer magnitude of the problem. When raising dwarf seahorses, you're dealing with a few dozen young at a time, but with the larger species you can easily end up with ten times that many fry on your hands. This means that your feeding problems will be ten times as great, and it will be ten times harder to maintain optimum water quality. Some simple multiplication will demonstrate this point. A young seahorse can consume 3000–4000 freshly hatched brine shrimp a day. Multiply that by 300 fry and you're faced with a staggering 1,200,000 brine shrimp nauplii daily! The average aquarist is just not up to such a colossal task.

Even so, the outlook is not as bleak as it seems. Once they make it past the infant stage, large seahorses are easy to maintain. The newborns grow remarkably fast, tripling in size in less than one month, so the trick is to keep them alive through those first few crucial weeks.

For a look at how this can be done, let's examine some of the problems facing the hobbyist who is interested in the challenge of raising large seahorses. The aquarist is apt to be confronted with his first crisis shortly after the delivery of the young. After emerging from its parent's pouch, the newborn's first instinct is to head for the surface to fill its air bladder. This accomplished, its second instinct is to anchor itself to something solid. Since it is surrounded by its siblings at this point, with dozens more soon to follow, the first hitching post it finds is very often the tail or snout of another baby seahorse. The same mistake is likely to be repeated again and again by the rest of the brood, creating a potentially dangerous situation. The entire spawn can eventually become hopelessly tangled in a writhing mass of tiny bodies. Snarled together tail-to-tail, head-to-tail, tail-to-snout, and so on, the babies are unable to feed and are doomed to slow starvation.

Should this deadly situation develop, it is easily cured. Gently disentangle the young seahorses, one by one if necessary. Once separated, carefully transfer the fry into a number of smaller aquariums. Besides breaking up their lethal log jam, isolating the young in several smaller tanks of their own is a good idea for many other reasons.

First, it protects them from their tankmates. Even the most harmless seahorse companions, which coexist splendidly with the adults, may prey on their young. Tiny anemones, small starfish, and shrimp will all take their toll if allowed to remain in the nursery tank(s).

Secondly, isolating the fry prevents cannibalism. Large seahorses eat virtually any live food that is small enough to be swallowed whole. If they are hungry enough, this includes newborn ponies. This is rarely a problem when they are well fed, but there's no sense in taking chances.

Most importantly, breaking the brood up into smaller groups gives the aquarist an insurance policy. Should disease break out in one of the nursery tanks, or if a pollution problem develops in one of them, there is no need for the rest of the spawn to be affected. These are very real possibilities when you are working with so many fry.

Once they are safely settled in their new quarters, raising the young becomes a matter of providing them with clean water and enough to eat. Maintaining decent water quality is a never-ending battle when you must contend with the metabolic wastes and oxygen demands of several dozen baby seahorses and the countless thousands of brine shrimp needed to feed them. For this reason it is a good idea to put an air-operated sponge filter in each nursery tank. Commonly known as "dirt magnets," these sponge filters will provided badly needed aeration and, in time, biological filtration. Even with the help of dirt magnets, frequent partial water changes are still the only way to prevent fouling of the water in your nursery tanks.

This is where the aquarist with access to the ocean has a big advantage. The ocean provides him with an inexhaustible source of clean water and live plankton, and if he can make regular trips to get them, his feeding and water control problems will be over.

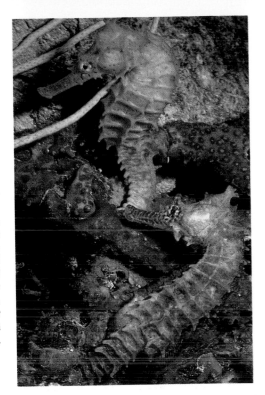

When breeding seahorses, it is strongly recommended that you keep the fry strictly by themselves. Even the smallest, most inoffensive tankmates—including adult seahorses—can wreak havoc among the newborns. In the giants, foals are past the critical stage at one month of age. After one year, they will be sexually mature, and shortly after this they reach their maximum length.

By comparison, the inland aquarist will have a far more difficult time meeting the requirements of a brood of large seahorses. Artificial salt water is expensive. So are the vast quantities of brine shrimp needed to feed hundreds of hungry little ponies. For these reasons, among others, the landlocked hobbyist who would like to breed seahorses is probably better off raising the dwarves (*Hippocampus zosterae*).

The inland aquarist who is serious about trying his hand at raising giant seahorses faces some hard decisions. His best chance for success is to literally reduce the problem to more manageable proportions. This means deciding how many newborn seahorses you can care for properly, and then culling mercilessly until you reach that number. The first step is to remove any stillborn babies (in some cases this can include one-third of the entire spawn). Next, weed out newborns that are still attached to yolk sacs and those with visible deformities. The chances of long term survival for fry with such handicaps are poor at best. Continue this process of elimination with the goal of selecting only the healthiest, most vigorous fry for further rearing.

If you feel you can only properly care for a dozen baby seahorses, so be it. The harsh truth is that it's far better to keep a few young seahorses in perfect health than to have a few hundred malnourished specimens, in water of rapidly deteriorating quality, that are certain to languish and die.

**DISEASES**

Like all fishes, seahorses are occasionally bothered by various ailments. When it comes to disease, prevention is always the best cure. If you select healthy specimens to begin with, feed them properly, and practice good aquarium management, the chances are good that you will never have to deal with many of the problems discussed in this chapter.

However, if disease should break out, early detection is the key to successful treatment. It is therefore important that you observe your specimens carefully every day in order to thoroughly acquaint yourself with their normal body markings and coloration.

Fortunately, the problem the seahorse keeper is most likely to encounter is easily detected and treated. This is gas formation, which commonly occurs in two different forms.

In some cases, actual bubbles of gas form just beneath the seahorse's skin. The bubbles most often form on its head, but they can also appear on other parts of its body. This condition can be cured by inserting a sharp, sterile needle just through the membrane of the bubble, taking care not to prick the seahorse's body. This will form a small puncture in the membrane, from which gas can then be expelled by gently massaging the sides of the bubble. This delicate operation is best performed underwater, holding the patient in one hand while puncturing the bubble and expelling the gas with your other hand. Once all of the gas has been released, the puncture wound should be disinfected by drying the area with sterile gauze or a cotton swab, and dabbing it with hydrogen peroxide, or a dilute solution of iodine, while holding the seahorse at the surface.

In other cases, the formation of gas in the brood pouches of male seahorses can be a recurrent problem. It apparently results when air is trapped within the brood pouch during the expulsion of the last of the young, or by the decomposition of stillborn young. In any case, it generally occurs soon after a pregnant male has delivered his brood. It is easily diagnosed by the swollen, bloated appearance of the pouch, which normally appears shrunken and wrinkled immediately after giving birth. This affliction is also readily treated by catching and holding the seahorse in one hand while locating the opening of the brood pouch with the other. You can easily detect the slot-like opening by carefully feeling for it at the upper, forward end of the pouch. Using your thumb or index finger to mark the opening, you can then insert a dull, sterile probe through the pouch orifice, thereby holding it open while you gently massage the sides of the pouch to release the gas. If the problem recurs, simply repeat the entire procedure.

Fin rot is another problem that sometimes afflicts seahorses in captivity. When this happens, the alert aquarist will notice that the fins of his seahorses are beginning to look frayed and ragged for no apparent reason. This damage is most obvious in the dorsal fin, which is almost always the first to be attacked. In its early stages, this disease is evident as a fine white line along the edge of the fin, which gradually advances towards the base of the fin until the fin rays become exposed, protruding like the ribs of a tattered umbrella. If the bacterial rot is left untreated, the entire fin will be destroyed and the body tissues of the seahorse will become infected, at which point it can no longer be saved. Early detection and treatment is crucial for curing fin rot. At the first sign of fin rot, Mildred Bellomy recommends submerging the infected seahorse in a 1 : 4000 solution of copper sulphate for one to two minutes. As she cautions, fishes undergoing this chemical

A seahorse afflicted with *Glugea*, a microsporidian parasite that causes white spot disease, is in trouble. The white spots are actually cysts filled with spores and can spread quickly over the body. When the cysts rupture, spores are released into the water and spread throughout the tank. *Glugea* is usually fatal; however, chemical baths, followed by coating the ulcerated cysts with an antibacterial agent, may help. Be that as it may, it is imperative that the infected seahorse be isolated as soon as possible to prevent spreading the disease.

bath should be watched closely and removed at the slightest sign of distress regardless of how much time has elapsed. A second bath should be administered in exactly the same manner 24 hours later. Along with these chemical dips, she also recommends that the infected fins be lightly swabbed with a good bacteriocidal agent, such as hydrogen peroxide, three to four times daily for a period of five to seven days. It may also be helpful to gradually lower the specific gravity of the aquarium water to about 1.020 during treatment, since fin rot is sometimes associated with high salinity.

Providing the fin rot is detected early, or is only a mild infection, seahorses usually recover completely following this regimen of treatment, and the damaged fins will be fully regenerated. Once again, I must stress the fact that the key to recovery is stopping fin rot in its tracks *before* the bacteria penetrates the tissue and the body of the seahorse becomes infected.

Seahorses are also subject to a number of parasitic diseases, some of which can be very serious. Fortunately for the aquarist, *Argulus*—the external parasite that is most often found on seahorses—is readily detected and cured. These small, flat-bodied parasites appear as semitransparent bumps, ranging from one-sixteenth to one-quarter inch in size, on the seahorse's head or the nape of its neck.

Better known as the sea louse, *Argulus* is a little bloodsucking horror equipped with a long, sharp proboscis that can pierce a seahorse's body with ease. Like so many diminutive Draculas, they have been observed sucking the blood flowing from the wounds made by their beaks. Fish parasitized by argulids naturally do everything possible to scrape them off, but their flattened bodies are able to cling tightly to their victims with special suction cups on their legs despite every effort of their hosts to dislodge them. Although these diabolical little vampires are only about the size of a water flea, heavily infested seahorses can become so irritated that they refuse to eat, and are further weakened by the loss of blood. In severe cases, death can result.

Luckily, if you purchase your seahorses from a pet dealer, you will probably never have to deal with the sinister sea louse, since they will have been removed by the collector prior to shipment. Needless to say, if you should ever happen to encounter a seahorse infested with these parasites, they should be removed at once. This can be accomplished by prying them loose with a tweezers, a dull pen knife blade, or any similar tool, while holding the seahorse submerged. Any wounds left by the argulids should be dried and disinfected using diluted iodine (one part iodine in nine parts of water) or other antibiotic. The "deloused" seahorse should then recover without any ill effects.

Learn to recognize your seahorses' normal behavior and coloration. Physical and behavioral changes often point to illness; and the sooner illness is recognized and treated, the better the chance of recovery.

Another parasite that sometimes plagues seahorses is an organism similar to the free-swimming *Ichthyophthirius multifiliis* which causes saltwater "ich." The first signs of ich are whitish pinpoints that appear on the host's body. These tiny spots are most easily seen on the transparent dorsal fin. The ciliated protozoan that causes them acts as a gill irritant and breaks down the skin on the seahorse's exoskeleton, which is usually when the aquarist first becomes aware of the disease. It reproduces extremely rapidly, both internally and by division, and seahorses quickly become heavily infected in the confines of the aquarium. Ich can be distinguished from *Glugea* because it causes respiratory distress and your seahorses will have difficulty breathing.

In 1978–79, a severe outbreak of this disease decimated the golden seahorses (*Hippocampus kuda*) from Hawaii. During the course of this epidemic, it was found that malachite green at 0.13 ppm is an effective cure for this parasite that can be used to treat the aquarium without damaging the bio-filter. To do this, you must prepare a stock solution by dissolving 100 mg of malachite green in 100 ml of deionized water. Adding one ml of this stock solution to every 20 gallons of salt water (or one-half ml per ten gallons) will then produce a concentration of 0.13 ppm in the aquarium. Malachite green dissipates fairly quickly, so you may need to administer more than one dose to bring about a cure.

It is important to note that there must be no copper present when this treatment is used, since copper combines with malachite green to produce a dangerous synergistic effect on fishes. In addition, it is recommended that this medication be used in *artificial salt water only*.

When this treatment is begun at the first sign of skin damage, the chances are good that your patient will make a complete recovery.

Fungus is an entirely different kind of problem that inexperienced aquarists sometimes confuse with white spot disease. It can be distinguished from *Glugea* by its fuzzy, cottonlike appearance, and the fact that it usually takes hold at the site of some injury such as a cut or a scrape. This cottony, local type of fungus can be treated by brushing it with a cotton swab dipped in Merthiolate and then coating the area with a paste made of sulfathiozole sodium mixed with castor oil. Isolation is not necessary, and the treatment should be continued, once a day, until the fungus has healed.

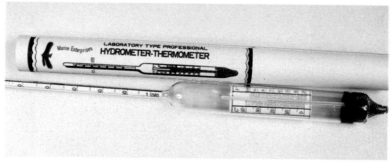

Proper water conditions, such as correct temperature and specific gravity, are imperative if the seahorses are to remain healthy. Therefore, a thermometer/-hydrometer is a necessity.

Fungus can also occur as a soft spot filled with pus. These spots can be treated by gently probing them with a sterile needle to open them up, removing the pus, and swabbing the area with Merthiolate.

In cold weather, seahorses are often collected with badly fungused areas on their bodies. Unlike local fungus, which is associated with an injury of some sort, this widespread fungus is apparently the result of chilling. The best way to treat it is by raising the temperature to 85°–90°F (29°–32°C) for most of the day, and repeating this heat treatment for several days at a time. (Be sure to increase the aeration along with the temperature.) With this type of fungus, it is a good idea to add one teaspoon of sulfathiazole sodium for each five gallons of water.

# Diseases

In addition to the previously described diseases, seahorses may also suffer due to the aquarist's mistakes. The worst of these is accidental poisoning as the result of toxic water. Toxic buildup in the aquarium has many causes—salt water coming in contact with metal or unsafe aquarium cements; improperly cured coral, shells, or rocks; contamination from carelessly placing your hands or fingers in the water; overcrowding or overfeeding; soaps, detergents, and other cleaning fluids and abrasives; fumes from insecticides, cigarette smoke, hairspray, paint, lacquer, gasoline, kerosene, etc.—but can often be attributed to negligence on the part of the aquarist.

Since the aquarist himself is at fault, a simple awareness of the above causes of toxic water on his part is all that is needed to avoid this problem. In short, toxic conditions can easily be prevented from occurring through common sense and good aquarium management.

Seahorses suffering from toxic water will stop feeding and show no interest in food. In later stages, they will be in obvious distress as shown by their labored breathing and rapid respirations, often literally gasping for air at the top of the tank. If they are not too far gone, they can be saved by simply removing them from the tank and placing them in freshly collected sea water or newly mixed artificial salt water. The source of the toxicity must then be removed or corrected, all the decorations and equipment must be cleaned thoroughly, and the aquarium water must be completely changed before the seahorses can be returned to their corral.

Aquarists unwittingly cause a different sort of problem when they introduce copepods such as *Cyclops* into the aquarium while feeding live foods. These minute crustaceans reproduce at a fantastic rate (over a year's time, the descendants from a single female may number over four billion) and can quickly transform your aquarium water into a copepod soup. When your seahorses try to breathe this copepod-infested water, their gill tufts can become hopelessly clogged by tangled masses of the tiny creatures, resulting in suffocation. As their respiration becomes increasingly labored, the seahorses will signal their distress by panting for breath and going through a series of color changes.

This problem is easily diagnosed by the cloudy or hazy appearance of the water. It can be treated by running a diatom filter continuously for several days, while adding three drops of methylene blue per gallon of water. The diatom filter physically removes the copepods, while the methylene blue further reduces their numbers and aids the seahorse's breathing. A complete water change is then called

# Diseases

for, and it may be necessary to carefully unclog the gill chambers of the affected seahorses with a wet cotton swab.

It is a good idea to maintain a hospital tank in your fish room for those times when you may have to doctor an ailing seahorse. It should be a small, well-aerated, all-glass aquarium equipped with a heater, some sort of hitching post, and nothing else. The ailing seahorse will not have to compete for food when it is provided with its own sick room, and the bare tank makes it easy to calculate the proper dosage of medications, as well as facilitating water changes. Most importantly, an isolation tank helps prevent the spread of disease through your display tanks, which is vital with highly infectious diseases like fin rot and *Glugea*. If you don't have a hospital tank, you must remember to turn off the canister filter when you treat your seahorses in their corral. Otherwise, the poly-filter pads and/or chemi-pure packs will promptly remove any medications that are added to the water.

When seahorses must be handled during the course of their treatment, be sure to grasp them by their bodies only, never by their heads or tails, taking special care not to injure their delicate dorsal fins. Remember that they should never be removed from the water for longer than a minute at any given time. Needless to say, the shorter the time a seahorse spends out of water, the better it will be.

Novice aquarists will be glad to learn that a multitude of commercially prepared medications for specific fish diseases are available from aquarium stores. No longer does the hobbyist have to prepare his own stock solutions of copper sulphate, malachite green, sulfathiazole sodium, etc. Many experienced hobbyists still prefer to prepare their own medications, since it saves money and their home remedies are tried and true cures that they have become experts at administering. Novice aquarists, however, will no doubt find it easier and more convenient to use the manufactured medications. Your aquarium dealer will be able to provide you with specific medications for fin rot, fungus, or saltwater "ich." Just follow the directions on the label, which will tell you the exact amount to add for your size aquarium, and you should have no trouble treating your seahorses.

When one of your seahorses happens to die (hopefully from natural causes due to old age), you can still preserve it for posterity. Simply arrange the body in a lifelike position and allow it to dry in the sun for several days. Once hardened, it can then be coated with shellac or clear acrylic spray to give it an attractive sheen, thus providing you with a long-lasting souvenir of your beloved pet.

The following books by T.F.H. Publications are available at pet shops everywhere.

**MINIATURE REEF AQUARIUM IN YOUR HOME by Dr. Cliff W. Emmens (TS-119)**
Provides a step-by-step description of miniature reef biology plus practical instruction and advice about setting up such an environment in the home. Hard cover, 128 pages.

# SUGGESTED READING

**MARINE FISHES AND INVERTEBRATES IN YOUR OWN HOME by Dr. Cliff W. Emmens (H-1103)**
The ultimate guide for both beginners and experts alike. Simple, direct language is used to instruct the marine hobbyist on how to set up and maintain a successful environment for his marine charges. Hard cover, 192 pages.

**DR. BURGESS'S ATLAS OF MARINE AQUARIUM FISHES by Dr. Warren E. Burgess, Dr. Herbert R. Axelrod, Raymond E. Hunziker III (H-1100)**
The most comprehensive identification index for marine fishes. Grouped by family, both popular aquarium inhabitants and oddball rarities are depicted in full color, with captions indicating range, size, and optimum tank conditions. This volume is the best reference around! Hard cover, 736 pages.

**MARINE COMMUNITY AQUARIUM by Dr. Leon P. Fann (H-1011)**
A stimulating introduction to the symbiotic associations that make the marine aquarium so fascinating. Emphasis is placed on keeping fish and invertebrates together in the miniature reef environment. Hard cover, 416 pages.

# Index